D1557787

Bayou Bend Collection and Gardens

MFA **H** *The Museum of Fine Arts, Houston*

THIS FIRST PRINTING IS DEDICATED TO MICHAEL K. BROWN (1953–2013),
curator of the Bayou Bend Collection and staff member of Bayou Bend
since 1980. He was a remarkable individual whose extraordinary
scholarship and connoisseurship was matched by his commitment
to excellence and by his kindness to everyone he encountered.

Writer: Remi S. Dyll
Designer: Phenon Finley-Smiley
Editors: Michael K. Brown, Bonnie A. Campbell,
Michelle Dugan, and Remi S. Dyll
Map: Tom Willcockson, Mapcraft.com
Printer: Masterpiece Litho, Inc.
10 9 8 7 6 5 4 3 2 1

Library of Congress Cataloguing-in-
Publication Data available upon request

ISBN: 978-0-89090-178-6
Printed in the United States of America

GENEROUS FUNDING FOR THIS
PUBLICATION IS PROVIDED BY:

GLORIA GARIC ANDERSON
CAROL AND LES BALLARD
KAY AND DAN ENGLISH
MARILYN LUMMIS

MARJORIE AND WALKER CAIN
ANNE AND TAFT SYMONDS

Contents

Introduction

A visit to Bayou Bend Collection and Gardens offers a unique blend of art, history, nature, and discovery. Nestled on the winding banks of Buffalo Bayou on fourteen acres of land in Houston's historic River Oaks neighborhood, Bayou Bend is the former home of legendary philanthropist and collector Ima Hogg (1882–1975). As visitors walk across a suspension bridge over the bayou, they enter the estate and encounter an oasis of formal gardens and woodlands surrounding a spacious mansion—hidden in the midst of Houston, one of the largest cities in the United States. Starting in the 1920s, Miss Hogg gradually assembled a significant collection of important art and antiques over the following five decades. Today, Bayou Bend houses the early American decorative arts and paintings collection of the Museum of Fine Arts, Houston, displayed in more than twenty-eight room settings and galleries, and recognized as one of the finest such collections in the country.

In 1973, Miss Hogg wrote, "Texas, an empire in itself, geographically and historically, sometimes seems to be regarded as remote or alien to the rest of our nation. I hope in a modest way Bayou Bend may serve as a bridge to bring us closer to the heart of an American heritage which unites us." Since then, it has continued to advance her vision and preserve her legacy. In 2010, the Museum opened the Lora Jean Kilroy Visitor and Education Center—designed to be a community gateway to the collection and gardens—adjacent to the estate. Today, Bayou Bend offers visitors much to explore: an outstanding museum of early American and 19th-century Texas decorative arts and paintings; gardens that preserve the historic Country Place Era of landscape design while promoting modern organic gardening; an education center that supports school, family, and adult learning; and a research library that focuses on American decorative arts and the material culture of 19th-century Texas.

Come discover Bayou Bend, the beautiful place with the romantic name—Houston's home for America's treasures.

The Hogg family, c. 1890. Left to right:
Ima, William, Thomas, Governor James
Stephen, Michael, and Sarah Ann Hogg

Ima Hogg: The Story of Bayou Bend's Founder

FAMILY FOUNDATIONS

"Our cup of joy is now overflowing. We have a daughter of as fine proportions and of as angelic mien as ever gracious nature favor a man with, and her name is Ima." These words, written by a proud father in the little East Texas town of Mineola in July 1882, heralded the debut of one of the most interesting women in Texas history. Thomas Elisha Hogg (1842–1880), uncle of the new baby, wrote the epic poem, *The Fate of Marvin*, in 1873 about the Civil War. She was named after the heroine of the story—Ima—a Scots-Irish diminutive of the name Imogene. She grew up to achieve national recognition as a patron of the arts, a philanthropist, and a major collector of early American antiques and paintings.

Little in her beginnings would suggest what the future held for Ima Hogg (1882–1975). She was the second child and only daughter of James Stephen (1851–1906) and Sarah Ann (née Stinson; 1854–1895) Hogg. The other children included William (1875–1930), older than Ima, and two younger brothers, Michael (1885–1941) and Thomas (1887–1949). In 1882, the Hoggs were living in modest circumstances, yet the family on both sides came from Southern plantation gentry. Sarah was the daughter of a Georgia planter who had moved his family to Texas after the Civil War.

James's family had come from Alabama and settled on a plantation near Rusk, Texas. His father, Joseph Lewis Hogg (1806–1862), a lawyer and planter, had been elected to the legislature of the Republic of Texas, fought in the Mexican-American War,

and served as a brigadier general in the Confederate Army during the Civil War. His father died at the head of his command in 1862, and his mother, Lucanda (1815–1863), died the following year, leaving Jim an orphan at age twelve. He and his two brothers were left with two older sisters to run the plantation. He largely educated himself and would study law, and by the time of his daughter's birth he was the owner and editor of a country newspaper. He became active in state politics and was elected attorney general in 1886. Four years later, Hogg was elected the first native-born governor of Texas.

At the age of eight, Ima moved to Austin with her family and into the 1856 Greek Revival-style Governor's Mansion. During these formative years, life in the mansion established Ima's lifelong interest in politics, history, and especially in American antiques.

Joseph Lewis Hogg, c. 1862

Hogg family children, c. 1895

9

Texas Governor's Mansion, 1888

Ima Hogg, 1896

Ima Hogg (right) in parade, Austin, 1903

She recalled later the thrill of sleeping in the huge four-poster bed that had belonged to Samuel "Sam" Houston (1793–1863), one of the most celebrated political figures of Texas. Her family was also influential in forming her interests. From her father, she acquired an abiding love of the state of Texas, a keen sense of public duty, a fascination with history, and an affection for flowers and trees. From her mother, she inherited a talent for music, a love of beauty, and a discerning eye that recognized good taste.

Sarah Hogg died in 1895 when Ima was thirteen. After leaving the Governor's Mansion that year, Jim Hogg practiced

Patton Place (now Varner-Hogg Plantation), 1901

Ima Hogg, c. 1920

Oil field, West Columbia, 1920

law and became prominent in national Democratic politics. He also speculated in the early oil industry in Texas. It was at this time that he purchased an antebellum Greek Revival-style house and plantation near West Columbia, Texas. While none of

of the children made Patton Place (now Varner-Hogg Plantation) their home, they each spent time there, including weekends entertaining visitors. Convinced that oil lay beneath the land's surface, he instructed his children not to sell their property until fifteen years after his death, which happened in 1906. As their father predicted, oil was discovered on the plantation in 1917, becoming the source of the family's vast wealth.

WHEN NOT COLLECTING

Ima Hogg showed a precocious interest in music. She had perfect pitch and by the age of three was playing the piano. After attending the University of Texas in Austin from 1899 to 1901, she departed for New York City to study music. This was followed by a three-year stint in Berlin beginning in 1907, where she continued to study piano and absorbed music at numerous concerts and operas. Although

she realized within several years that she was not destined for a career as a concert pianist, her commitment to music continued, and in 1913 she was one of the founders of what was to become the Houston Symphony. Throughout her life, she was a tireless worker on the symphony's behalf, serving twice as president.

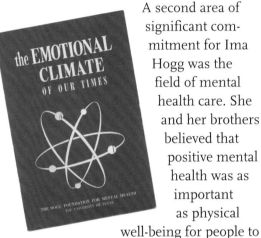

A second area of significant commitment for Ima Hogg was the field of mental health care. She and her brothers believed that positive mental health was as important as physical well-being for people to reach their full potential and enjoy productive lives. In 1929, she helped found the Houston Child Guidance Center, one of the first such organizations in the country dedicated to treatment and prevention of childhood behavioral problems. She was instrumental in arranging the estate of her eldest brother, William, to be used to create the Hogg Foundation for Mental Hygiene (now Hogg Foundation for Mental Health) at the University of Texas. Since its inception in 1940, the foundation has been a national leader in the medical profession; at her death, the bulk of her estate was bequeathed to it.

Governor Hogg discussed the educational needs of Texans with Will and Ima during 1905–06. The Hoggs promoted publicly funded education for all citizens from kindergarten through postgraduate study.

They followed the progress of Houston's Rice Institute (now Rice University), which opened in 1912. In the 1920s, Miss Hogg underwrote the first music program offered by the institute. During the 1940s, she served on the Houston Independent School District's Board of Education, pledging to represent "all the citizens of Houston, regardless of class, color, or creed." She championed equal pay for equal work for all—man or woman, black or white. She also organized a school for children with special needs, established a visiting teacher program, and advocated for after-school child care and classroom instruction in art and music.

An accomplished woman of wide-ranging interests, Ima Hogg did not limit her endeavors to music, mental health care, and public education. In later years, she also became involved in historical preservation and restoration, beginning with her parents' first home in Quitman, Texas, and continuing with Varner-Hogg Plantation. A major restoration project involved a complex of Texas-German buildings named Winedale Historical Center in Fayette County given to the University of Texas as an outdoor museum and center for the study of 19th-century German culture in Texas in 1965. In the process of completing the project, Miss Hogg became interested in the furniture made by the Texas-Germans. Today, Bayou Bend actively acquires such furniture and related decorative arts.

Houston Symphony meeting, Bayou Bend, c. 1935

Ima Hogg and Wayne Bell, Winedale Historical Center, c. 1967

Hogg Foundation publication, 1959

Ima Hogg, c. 1940

Armchair (right) inspired purchase of armchair (left) in 1920

THE COLLECTING DISEASE

*"It is said that collecting is a disease.
I think I had it from childhood."*
—Ima Hogg, August 1973

Office interior,
Hogg Brothers, Houston,
c. 1928

Despite her many important civic contributions, Ima Hogg is perhaps best known for assembling a remarkable collection of Americana, one of the finest in the country. Just prior to World War I, she began to purchase English antiques. Will Hogg kept an apartment on Park Avenue in New York City, and while on a visit there in 1920, Miss Hogg sat for her portrait in the studio of Wayman Adams (1883–1959). She admired an armchair in the room and asked the artist about its origins. She was intrigued to learn that it was American, dating from the mid-18th century; shortly thereafter, she purchased a similar example. She perceived that through a piece of early American furniture, one could explore and interpret the nation's history and culture. At the time, appreciation for American decorative arts was a relatively new field of interest, being that America had only celebrated its centennial in 1876 and not many yet considered American objects as something to study and preserve. In contrast, the much older English and European decorative arts had been avidly collected for many years.

Soon after her 1920 purchase of the armchair, Ima Hogg became one of the first serious collectors of early American furniture, beginning what became a life-long collecting passion. Along with Will, she read everything she could find on the topic, including early-20th-century auction catalogues that included pieces identified as American. They also got to know the principal dealers in the field (primarily based in New York at that time) and befriended the most knowledgeable scholar in the field, Charles O. Cornelius, an associate curator at the Metropolitan Museum of Art (which opened its American Wing in 1924). As the 1920s progressed, Will Hogg assembled a notable collection

of paintings by Frederic Remington, later given by Ima to the Museum of Fine Arts, Houston. During this time, Miss Hogg's collecting was not limited to Americana. She was also interested in contemporary art, particularly works on paper—drawings, watercolors, and prints. By her account, on a trip to the Soviet Union in 1929, her eyes were opened by avant-garde art. On her way home, she bought works by Paul Klee and Pablo Picasso. Her art collection eventually would include works by German Expressionists whose interest in music reflected hers. Moreover, summer visits to New Mexico made her aware of the arts of the Southwest American Indians, and in the 1920s and 1930s, she assembled a comprehensive collection of pottery, kachina dolls, and silver jewelry. Each of these collections was given to the Museum, the contemporary art in 1939 and the Indian art in 1944.

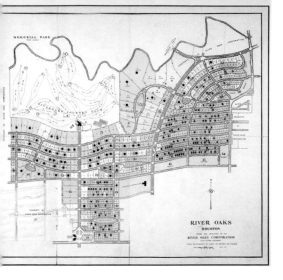

Plan of River Oaks, 1930

The mansion was completed in 1928. The three siblings lived there together for only a short time. Mike married in 1929, and Will died the next year. Ima would live at Bayou Bend until 1965.

Houston Post-Dispatch, August 26, 1928

Houston Post-Dispatch

HOUSTON, TEXAS, SUNDAY, AUGUST 26, 1928

FIRST PICTURES OF MISS IMA HOGG'S HOME IN RIVER OAKS

A FAMILY HOME: BAYOU BEND

The Hogg Brothers firm, which dealt in oil, agriculture, real estate, and other interests, developed the planned garden community, River Oaks, in Houston in the 1920s and went on to build the adjacent Homewoods addition, selecting a prime lot for themselves. Miss Hogg wanted a name that would suggest "contentment, quiet, country" and decided on Bayou Bend for the curve of Buffalo Bayou that borders the property on two sides.

Ima and two of her two brothers, Will and Mike, commissioned Houston architect John F. Staub (1892–1981), with the assistance of associate architect Birdsall P. Briscoe (1876–1971), to design a mansion. While she desired a neo-Palladian plan, she felt a brick Georgian elevation was not appropriate for the climate of Houston. Instead she and Staub chose a pink stucco exterior and fitted it with cast-iron details found in the architecture of New Orleans and the Gulf Coast, dubbed by Miss Hogg as a "Latin Colonial" style. On the interior, Staub combined 18th-century and early-19th-century styles to create harmonious settings for the family's growing antiques and art collection.

John F. Staub, c. 1948

Ima Hogg's collecting of Americana virtually stopped in the 1930s as she focused first on setting up the Hogg Foundation and then later on the development of the estate's extensive gardens, as she was an avid gardener and horticulturist (see p. 72). Although she continued to refine her collections of Southwest American Indian artifacts and modern

Ima Hogg and River Oaks Garden Club members, Clio Garden, c. 1958

Library (now Pine Room), c. 1930

First docent class, Ima Hogg and Jonathan Fairbanks, Philadelphia Hall, 1961

European art, it was not until the 1940s that her attention returned to collecting Americana.

THE COLLECTION GROWS

Later in her life, Ima Hogg explained that the idea of one day transforming Bayou Bend from a private home to a public

Houston Chronicle, December 30,1956

Ima Hogg, Katharine Prentis Murphy, and John F. Staub, Murphy Room, 1959

house museum was first suggested in the early 1940s by Ray L. Dudley, a trustee of the Museum of Fine Arts, Houston. As an extension of the fine arts museum, Bayou Bend would provide sufficient space to exhibit her American collection and allow for its future growth. The concept seems to have reignited her interest in the field, and in 1943 she went to New York and purchased several fine chairs.

Beginning in the early 1950s, Ima Hogg's purchases increased in scope and quantity. During this decade she acquired many of the collection's finest works from 18th-

century colonial America. Also at this time, she began to collect American paintings from the same period, by artists such as John Singleton Copley, Charles Willson Peale, and Gilbert Stuart.

SHOWPLACE FOR ART

Hogg Home To Museum

Bayou Bend, the palatial home of Miss Ima Hogg has been given to the Museum of Fine Arts to serve as a decorative arts museum.

The announcement was made by Francis G. Coates, Museum board president.

Miss Hogg will continue to reside in the house. It will be several years before the house and its collections will be opened as a museum.

bridge will be built to permit access.

In making the gift Miss Hogg said, "I have been collecting and assembling examples of early American furniture and other objects used by our colonial forefathers. This has been done with serious intent, always with the idea of preserving such treasures for Texas."

Originally built by Miss Hogg and her late brothers Mike and Will Hogg in the lat...

FROM MANSION TO MUSEUM

Evidence suggests that Ima Hogg's concept of keeping the collection in her home began to crystallize by the mid-1950s. Over the years the Hoggs had formed close ties with the Museum of Fine Arts, Houston. In fact, they were instrumental in securing the institution's original building in 1924. In 1957, Ima Hogg deeded Bayou Bend to the Museum with the understanding that a public collection be created. In its preparation, she began the complex process that would convert her home into a museum. John Staub returned to Bayou Bend to assist Miss Hogg in reconfiguring the rooms to better display the collection. Additionally, so as not to disrupt her River Oaks' neighbors to the south, a pedestrian suspension bridge was built over the bayou that provided visitor access on the west side of the property. Last, the garage was renovated to make a reception area and a small lecture hall for a core group of docents.

By 1965, Bayou Bend's conversion into a museum was virtually complete. David B. Warren, the first curator, was hired (he became founding director emeritus in 2003), and Miss Hogg moved from

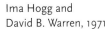
Ima Hogg at dedication of Bayou Bend, 1966

Ima Hogg and David B. Warren, 1971

Ima Hogg, 1973

the house to a nearby high-rise apartment. When Bayou Bend was formally dedicated and opened to the public in 1966 as the American decorative arts and paintings branch of the Museum of Fine Arts, Houston, she remarked, "It is my hope the objects in the collection will be appreciated not only for their aesthetic quality, but for their historic significance. While I shall continue to love Bayou Bend and everything here, in one sense I have always considered I was holding Bayou Bend only in trust for this day."

She would continue to be involved with acquiring decorative arts and paintings for the collection and supported the addition of three entire new room settings.

While visiting London in 1975, she died at the age of ninety-three. Miss Hogg left a remarkable collection to the Museum, along with spectacular gardens, so not only a few but all could enjoy and learn.

Timeline of American Style

The Bayou Bend Collection features decorative arts and paintings representing seven periods in American style history spanning from about 1620 to 1876. This timeline focuses on the design of chairs, silver, and case furniture, and shows how the look of the objects changed over time.

c. 1620–1690
LATE RENAISSANCE (JACOBEAN/17ᵀᴴ CENTURY)

- Heavy proportions
- Classical architectural elements
- Stylized ornamentation
- Shallow geometric and floral carvings
- Straight lines
- Bright colors
- **1607**, Jamestown establishes first English settlement in America
- **1620**, English Pilgrims establish Plymouth Colony in Massachusetts
- **1698**, King William III and Queen Mary II crowned in England

c. 1690–1730
EARLY BAROQUE (WILLIAM AND MARY)

- Vertical, thin lines
- Lavish ornament based on cabriole (S-curved) lines
- Natural, exotic, and classical ornament
- Mix of light and dark surfaces
- Japanning (furniture decoration inspired by Asian lacquer)
- **1698**, First public library in America in Charles Town, South Carolina
- **1698**, Anglo population in America reaches 275,000
- **1718**, France founds New Orleans

c. 1730–1755
LATE BAROQUE (QUEEN ANNE)

- Cabriole (S-curved) lines
- Classical proportions
- Delicate, shallow ornament
- Restrained use of ornament and color
- Japanning on furniture
- Chinoiserie (decoration dominated by Chinese or pseudo-Chinese ornamental motifs)
- **1730**, Construction begins on Independence Hall in Philadelphia
- **1738** and **1743**, Excavation begins at Roman ruins

C. 1755–1790
ROCOCO
(CHIPPENDALE)

- Curvaceous forms
- Natural-looking carving and engraving
- Asymmetrical and organic ornament
- Contrasting textures
- Claw-and-ball foot
- Cabriole leg
- Pierced splats on chairs
- French, Chinese, and Gothic novelties
- **1754–1763**, French and Indian War
- **1775–1783**, American Revolution
- **1787**, United States Constitution is adopted

C. 1790–1810
NEOCLASSICAL
(FEDERAL)

- Classical proportions and ornament
- Geometric partitioning
- Straight lines
- Delicate scale
- Symmetry
- Inlay on furniture
- Shallow carving and engraving
- Contrasts of light and dark
- **1800**, Capitol moves from Philadelphia to Washington, D.C.
- **1803**, United States purchases Louisiana from France

C. 1810–1845
GRECIAN
(EMPIRE)

- Archaeological emphasis
- Heavy forms
- Plain and dark veneers on furniture
- Gilding
- Paw feet and animal heads
- Sculptural carving
- Vibrant colors
- Bold textures
- **1812–1815**, War of 1812
- **1836**, Republic of Texas is established; Houston is founded

C. 1845–1876
ROCOCO REVIVAL
(EARLY VICTORIAN)

- Curvaceous lines
- Sculptured surfaces
- Extravagant and realistic naturalism
- Asymmetry
- Scroll feet and cabriole legs
- High-relief ornament
- Laminated (layered) wood on furniture
- **1845**, Congress annexes Texas as 28th state of the Union
- **1846–1848**, Mexican-American War
- **1861–1865**, American Civil War

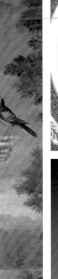

The Bayou Bend Collection traces the evolution of decorative style in America from the early 17th century to the late 19th century, and is displayed in elegant room settings throughout the mansion.

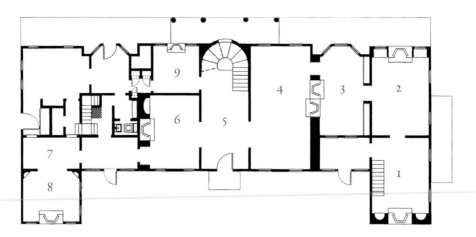

First Floor

1	Murphy Room	6	Dining Room
2	Massachusetts Room		*Chillman Suite:*
3	Pine Room	7	Chillman Foyer
4	Drawing Room	8	Chillman Parlor
5	Philadelphia Hall	9	Belter Parlor

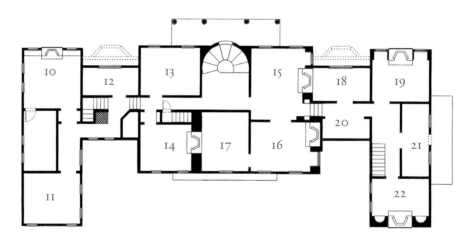

Second Floor

10	Music Room	17	Folk Art Room
11	McIntire Bedroom	18	Ceramics Study Room
12	Michael K. Brown Metals Study Room	19	Federal Parlor
13	Chippendale Bedroom	20	Texas Alcove
14	Maple Bedroom	21	Texas Room
	Queen Anne Suite:	22	Newport Room
15	Queen Anne Sitting Room		
16	Queen Anne Bedroom		

Bayou Bend Collection and Gardens is home to the early American decorative arts and paintings collection of the Museum of Fine Arts, Houston. More than 2,500 objects are on view in twenty-eight room settings and galleries. The objects, made or used in America between 1620 and 1876, include furniture, paintings, prints, metals, ceramics, textiles, glass, and sculpture.

From the time Ima Hogg acquired her first piece of American furniture in 1920, she had what she later described as "an unaccountable compulsion to make an American collection for some Texas museum." In 1957, Miss Hogg gave Bayou Bend and her collection to the Museum. She spent the following nine years transforming Bayou Bend from private residence to public museum, creating room settings that suggest early American interiors from particular periods. In 1966, Bayou Bend opened to the public and was soon recognized locally and nationally as a cultural treasure.

Ima Hogg considered the collection to be a work in progress and encouraged those following her to add objects or substitute better examples as appropriate. The collection has grown by more than one-third since her death in 1975 at the age of ninety-three.

Ima Hogg wanted Bayou Bend to "serve as a bridge to bring us closer to the heart of an American heritage which unites us." The following pages highlight the interiors and room settings, beginning with the earliest period in colonial American history and extending until just after the American Civil War.

Ima Hogg in Drawing Room,
c. 1966

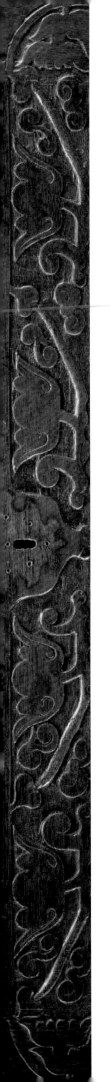

THE MURPHY ROOM

Named for Ima Hogg's friend and fellow collector Katharine Prentis Murphy who closely advised her on its creation, the Murphy Room was dedicated in 1959 and was Miss Hogg's first effort at creating a museum interior at Bayou Bend. The painted, black-and-white checkerboard floor was inspired by some found in late-17th-century Boston portraits, which scholars now believe represented painted canvas floorcloths, rather than painted boards.

The room setting displays the oldest objects in the collection dating from the Late Renaissance (1620–1690) and Early Baroque (1690–1730) periods. Houses in that era were sparsely outfitted with only rudimentary furnishings. A family would be lucky to have one armchair, or what was called a "great chair," which was often reserved for the father or an important guest. In the 17th century, the family's most esteemed possessions, including textiles, were kept in a cupboard or chest. The cupboard was a form owned by few, a showpiece of wealth, used for storage as well as to display costly imported tin-glazed earthenware, salt-glazed stoneware, and pewter.

THE PINE ROOM

This room was originally a library, the walls lined with floor-to-ceiling bookshelves. When Ima Hogg transformed the library into a museum interior in the 1960s, she covered the shelves with new pine paneling patterned after mid-18th-century woodwork that she admired in a period room installed at the Metropolitan Museum of Art.

Today, the Pine Room displays many objects in the Early Baroque style (1690–1730). High chests of drawers, similar to Bayou Bend's Boston example, began to appear during this period. They were made by a new, more skilled class of craftsmen called cabinetmakers who used dovetailed construction and often dramatic, veneered surfaces. The distinguished portraits by John Smibert, the first major art celebrity in the American colonies, retain their original carved frames.

The Queen Anne Suite

Several of Bayou Bend's rooms today reflect Miss Hogg's taste and arrangement when she lived in the house, including these two spaces that formed her personal suite on the second floor.

QUEEN ANNE SITTING ROOM

The fireplace wall paneling in the room is one of the historical elements installed in the house during its 1920s construction, and dates to the third quarter of the 18th century; the blue-green paint is based on evidence of its original color. Ima Hogg chose this room to house her collection of English and Continental tin-glazed earthenwares with their distinctive, powdered manganese ground; several examples adorn the mantel. John Singleton Copley, the finest artist of colonial America, painted the pastel portrait of Mrs. Joseph Henshaw hanging above the fireplace. Miss Hogg realized Copley's superior skill and importance, acquiring ten of his works for the collection. The large portrait of Mrs. Samuel McCall, Sr. is by Robert Feke, the first major native-born artist of the colonies.

The room is furnished with examples in the Late Baroque style (1730–55). One of Bayou Bend's great masterpieces, the Boston-made card table, features a late-18th-century needlework top, a design element that was rarely incorporated on card tables, which typically had a wood surface. Only a few such tables have survived the centuries. One of the highlights of the collection is the rare, early-18th-century Boston-made high chest of drawers ornamented with painted decoration, gilding, and molded gesso elements, called Asian lacquerwork, reflecting the popularity of chinoiserie in the 18th century.

QUEEN ANNE BEDROOM

The Queen Anne Bedroom incorporates period 18th-century woodwork and flooring. Above the fireplace hangs a portrait of William Holmes from Charleston, South Carolina, by the colonial painter John Wollaston. The New England armchair with a rush seat was the very one that inspired Miss Hogg to start her collection of American furniture in 1920 (see p. 12); she was able to acquire it in 1968. The high chest of drawers from Eastern Massachusetts is covered with a figured veneer and ornamented with a stylized shell on the central drawer; blue-and-white delft (tin-glazed earthenware) objects from England are displayed on top. The Pennsylvania spice box, suspended at the right of the bed, once stored small valuables and precious spices in an assortment of drawers, which are revealed when the door is unlocked.

THE DRAWING ROOM

The largest space in the house, the Drawing Room, reflects the Georgian architecture of mid-18th-century American interiors. The design for many of the architectural details is borrowed from a 1769 room at Shirley Plantation in Virginia. Today, the room is a gallery of outstanding furniture in the Rococo style (1755–90) made in cities along the Atlantic seaboard from Boston to Charleston. Iconic pieces in the collection, the Newport desk-and-bookcase and the bureau table (see pp. 34–35) reflect the most significant design element to originate in 18th-century America— the block-and-shell motif, created and popularized by Newport craftsmen.

Three of early America's most distinguished artists are represented in the room. Above the mantel hangs a painting of John Vaughan by Gilbert Stuart, the primary portraitist of post-Revolutionary America renowned for his many depictions of George Washington. Across the room hangs a portrait of Mrs. Paul Richard painted by John Singleton Copley. An American masterpiece, the highly sophisticated group portrait by Charles Willson Peale shows the artist painting a portrait of his wife, Rachel. Behind him, their daughter Angelica, as an allegorical muse of painting, guides her father's brush with one hand, while pointing to heaven with the other.

THE PHILADELPHIA HALL

The wide central entrance hall in the Neoclassical style visually extends through the house to the gardens beyond. Its curving staircase echoes the elliptical shape of the far wall and may have been inspired by the one in the Governor's Mansion in Austin where Ima Hogg lived as a child. Painted by Houston artist Robert C. Joy in 1971, the portrait of Ima Hogg shows her sitting in a Philadelphia armchair surrounded by much-loved objects from her collection.

Philadelphia Hall is so named because its furniture in the Rococo style (1755–90) was made in that city. The high chest of drawers reflects a unique, iconic American form that would have originally been used to store clothing and bedding in a bed chamber. The elaborately carved, naturalistic elements are typical of the Rococo style. To the right of the staircase, a card table, another popular form in 18th-century Philadelphia, is surmounted by an English pier glass.

THE MASSACHUSETTS ROOM

The Massachusetts Room's dramatic blue walls reflect the color Ima Hogg chose in 1928 when the house was new, inspired by a piece of 18th-century Portuguese chintz. The room showcases Salem and Boston furniture in the Rococo style (1755–90). The sophisticated objects reflect the greater material wealth of colonists on the eve of the American Revolution in comparison to their 17th-century ancestors.

The double chair-back design of the settee was a Boston specialty. Bayou Bend's example is accompanied by eight matching side chairs, a rarity to have survived en suite. The turret-top table with scalloped edge was especially made for a tea service, such as the English soft paste porcelain by the Worcester Porcelain Company displayed on it today. Above hangs a portrait of three-year-old John Gerry of Marblehead, Massachusetts, by Joseph Badger. His coat, passed down through descendants with the portrait, survives in the Bayou Bend Collection.

THE CHIPPENDALE BEDROOM

Originally a guestroom in the house, the Chippendale Bedroom reflects a mid-18th-century bedchamber with period-appropriate architectural details, furnished with Rococo-style (1755–90) pieces from Salem and the Boston area. The room also houses a fine collection of prints relevant to the American Revolution. The desk-and-bookcase is exceptional for its bombé sides combined with a serpentine front. The desk functioned essentially as its owner's office, housing letters, accounts, and books. Fashionable decor of the period required that window curtains, upholstery, and bed hangings be made to match. The fully dressed bedstead requiring approximately sixty yards of wool would have been the major expense of the bedroom mainly because all fabrics were imported to the colonies at the time.

In 1767, Charles Willson Peale, then an aspiring artist, traveled to London to study under the renowned American-born painter Benjamin West. The following year he painted Bayou Bend's ambitious portrait of a young boy in a fashionable London interior. Before the early 1800s, girls and boys were outfitted alike in dresses, until after age six, boys wore breeches or trousers; also, pink and blue were used interchangeably for both until the early 1900s.

THE NEWPORT ROOM

This room's paneling is based on the parlor of the 1748 Hunter House in Newport, Rhode Island. The city, at the head of Narragansett Bay, was a thriving seaport and a major center of furniture production during the 18th century. The distinguished Goddard and Townsend families of Newport cabinetmakers interpreted the Rococo (1755–90) style in a restrained and distinctive fashion closely allied to the earlier Late Baroque style, influencing other local cabinetmakers.

The carved, stylized shell is synonymous with Newport furniture, as is concave and convex blocking, both of which are evident in the room's mahogany desk-and-bookcase. A round card table in front of the fireplace was a British tradition since the 17th century. Bayou Bend's example was made for the merchant Thomas Robinson, whose house was four blocks from John Goddard's home and workshop, lending to its Newport attribution. Easy chairs were often found in 18th-century Newport bedchambers. The dramatic but practical "wings" shielded the sitter from drafts or the heat from the fireplaces.

THE MAPLE BEDROOM

The Maple Bedroom represents an early-19th-century country bedchamber and is a setting for vernacular objects common to rural areas in Massachusetts, Connecticut, New York, and Pennsylvania. The furnishings suggest several previous generations of occupation. The room includes a fireplace surround of 18th-century style paneling and a cornice outlined by a 19th-century style pinecone-and-leaf stenciled border.

Two important paintings are on display. Over the fireplace is *Peaceable Kingdom* by Edward Hicks, a Quaker minister and a renowned 19th-century artist. Illustrating a biblical prophecy that foretold a time of peace, wisdom, and understanding, the allegory shows a trusting child and gentle animals, while William Penn and American Indians sign the 1682 treaty that allowed the Quakers to establish a community in Pennsylvania. At the time famed portraitist Ralph Earl painted Dr. Mason Fitch Cogswell, the professional practice of medicine had begun to flourish in America. Medical textbooks on the shelves behind the sitter hint that the Yale-educated doctor was among the more qualified members of his profession.

The leopard with the harmless kid laid down,
And not one savage beast was seen to frown.

L'Humilité

INNOCENTIA

The wolf did with the lambkin dwell in peace,
His grim carnivrous nature there did cease.

The lion with the fatling on did move,
A little child was leading them in love;

MEEKNESS
INNOCENCE

When the great PENN his famous treaty made
With INDIAN chiefs beneath the elm tree's shade.

THE DINING ROOM

The furnishings in the Dining Room are mainly in the New York Neoclassical style (1790–1810). The pale green ceiling, cupboard, and the white ceiling plasterwork (see pp. 48–49) reflect many of the style's characteristics. The shimmering, gold-leaf canvas wall covering, designed in 1927–28 by New York artist William MacKay, is hand-painted with Texas dogwood branches, peonies, and garden creatures such as field mice and butterflies.

A room designated for dining emerged in wealthy homes after the American Revolution, resulting in two new furniture forms: the banquet-sized dining table and the sideboard. The table is set for the soup course with a Chinese export porcelain service, probably made c. 1800 for Philadelphia merchant Thomas Willing. The dessert course is set up on the sideboard, and the secretary holds other pieces. Adorned with classical motifs, the porcelain is displayed alongside American and English silver and major pieces of export porcelain. Reflecting the taste and arrangement of Ima Hogg, the cupboard displays 18th-century English salt-glazed stoneware and 19th-century ceramics made by Spode.

THE McINTIRE BEDROOM

The furniture in this room was made in Salem and Boston, Massachusetts, and nearby Portsmouth, New Hampshire, all in the Neoclassical style (1790–1810). The room is named after Samuel McIntire, the renowned architect and woodcarver who is identified with exquisitely carved furniture from Salem. The bedroom is carpeted and wallpapered in a pattern-on-pattern manner that McIntire would recognize. The bedstead is hung with chinoiserie chintz, with matching curtains.

Some pieces reflect the role of women in the early years of the new republic. Among new furniture forms was the worktable. Fitted with storage for needle cases and thread-winders, it held a lady's projects in the silk bag suspended from the frame. On the walls are examples of needlework by young girls attending boarding schools.

THE FEDERAL PARLOR

The Federal Parlor showcases the decorative arts of the urban centers of New England and the mid-Atlantic states during the Neoclassical period (1790–1810). The parlor was the room in which the family drank tea, played cards, danced, and entertained guests. The mantel signed by Robert Wellford of Philadelphia, features allegorical figures, bowknots, and swags. The painting above by Charles Willson Peale depicts a pastoral scene with a Philadelphia-area manor house in the distance.

Like the McIntire Bedroom, this parlor reflects the rising prominence of women in society. The lady's desk, attributed to the renowned shop of John and Thomas Seymour in Boston, has a writing flap and is fitted with compartments and drawers to hold letters behind the tambour doors. Above the desk hangs a portrait of Sarah Trumbull painted by her husband, John Trumbull, one of America's most important artists.

THE MUSIC ROOM

This setting, in the early Grecian style (1810–20), suggests a prosperous time in America (see pp. 56–57). Reflecting Ima Hogg's musical interests, both as a pianist and a founder of the Houston Symphony, the square piano was made by Gibson and Davis of New York. This popular instrument was considered especially suitable for ladies, who frequently were recorded in diaries as playing them while singing. They were often accompanied by a gentleman amateur playing the flute, such as the American-made example in its original box on the card table. Some of the chairs have curved backs and legs based on the klismos form borrowed from ancient Greece.

After the Revolution, the United States began to trade directly with China. This is represented by a Chinese export porcelain tea and coffee service decorated with America's Great Seal and the bamboo armchair made for the West at the right of the fireplace. The American fascination was not limited to China. One of the most striking features of the room is the French reproduction panoramic wallpaper, which depicts scenes of India. The floor is laid with reproduction wall-to-wall wool carpeting—an expensive practice that was limited to the wealthiest members of American society at the time.

THE CHILLMAN SUITE

The Chillman Suite highlights furniture mostly made in the mid and later periods of the Grecian style (1810–45). The rooms were named to honor Dorothy Dawes Chillman, wife of James H. Chillman, Jr., the first director of the Museum. She was an interior decorator and close friend of Miss Hogg, who helped her develop Bayou Bend's period rooms in the 1950s and 1960s.

CHILLMAN FOYER

One first enters the foyer and discovers a monumental gilded mahogany sideboard, with a luscious still-life painting of vegetables above by James Peale. Working in Philadelphia, Peale popularized still-life painting in the United States, a country in which art patrons previously preferred portraits. The gilt pier glass is suspended above a New York table, with a rare, painted klismos chair designed by Benjamin Henry Latrobe at the left. Latrobe's interpretation of the Greek form draws on the designs of Thomas Hope of England and represents an early—or perhaps the earliest—documented example of the style in America. Latrobe designed furniture for many notable homes, including the White House.

CHILLMAN PARLOR

In the adjacent parlor, the walls are hung with portraits by accomplished 19th-century American artists, such as Rembrandt Peale and Thomas Sully. The reproduction wall-to-wall carpeting is based on a period example, while painted valances above the curtains date from c. 1835.

The center table holds a silver tea and coffee service by the Baltimore silversmith Samuel Kirk and porcelain teawares by the Philadelphia manufacturer William Ellis Tucker; these craftsmen produced stylish goods for urban customers, demonstrating that by this period the United States was capable of competing with fashionable products from Europe. As music was often played at home during this era, the parlor includes a beautiful harp along with a New York side chair that features a harp design in its back.

THE BELTER PARLOR

The furnishings in the Belter Parlor reflect the Rococo Revival style (1845–70), the most popular design of the mid-Victorian era. The room takes its name from John Henry Belter, a German-trained cabinetmaker who was a leading manufacturer in New York City during the 1850s. He patented a method using steam pressure to mold and laminate wood, creating dramatically curved surfaces that could be deeply carved. Belter's factory made Bayou Bend's matching set of furniture: two sofas, two armchairs, four side chairs, center table, and étagère, a new furniture form used to display small objects that revealed a family's taste, education, and elegance. The glass chandelier is a gasolier that originally burned natural gas produced from coal. The fireplace is set off by the marble mantelpiece carved with a profusion of birds, flowers, and fruit.

THE FOLK ART ROOM

During Ima Hogg's time in the house, this interior accommodated her bath and dressing room. Following her death in 1975, her sister-in-law, Alice Hogg Hanszen, underwrote the renovation of the room to recognize Miss Hogg's many interests and civic contributions. Since the opening of the Lora Jean Kilroy Visitor and Education Center in 2010, that concept has been incorporated into the Hogg Family Legacy Room (see p. 95), which was underwritten by Mrs. Hanszen's niece, Museum life trustee Alice C. Simkins.

Whereas most of the Bayou Bend Collection reflects the products of urban and urbane societies, this space exhibits a range of painted furniture, art, wood sculpture, weathervanes, and pottery that can be grouped under the all-encompassing term "folk art," emanating from a myriad of sources and societies. Often, these objects served a practical function as well as an artistic one. The early-19th-century cupboard from Berks County, Pennsylvania, was designed to store and display dishes and glassware, and was an important feature of the Pennsylvania German kitchen; the artisan painted Bayou Bend's example with fanciful designs and grained decoration, making it not only functional but a work of art. Similarly, the room's exuberantly decorated pair of artist-signed, grain-painted doors complements the cupboard; functional in purpose, they are believed to have been made for an Odd Fellows Meetinghouse in Saugerties, New York, around 1850–60.

THE TEXAS ROOM

The surge of German immigrants in Texas in the 1840s and 1850s brought with them the Biedermeier style, a furniture aesthetic that employed simple and comfortable designs along with fine craftsmanship. Most of the furniture in the room today was made in central Texas in the mid-19th century. Objects attributed to the accomplished cabinetmaker Johann Michael Jahn of New Braunfels, Texas, include the pair of side chairs, serpentine-back sofa, and footstool. A worktable from central Texas stands near the sofa and above hangs *West Cave on the Pedernales*, painted by German immigrant Hermann Lungkwitz in 1883.

Filling the cupboards are examples of Texian Campaigne ceramics made in Staffordshire, England, for the international market to commemorate the Texas War of Independence (1835–36) and later the Mexican-American War (1846–48). There are references to heroes of these two wars, especially General Zachary Taylor, on glass flasks and other ceramics on view. The cedar paneling with Gothic arches is based on woodwork from a house built in Independence, Texas, around 1850, which prompts a small assemblage of objects that are indicative of the mid-19th century's Gothic Revival aesthetic.

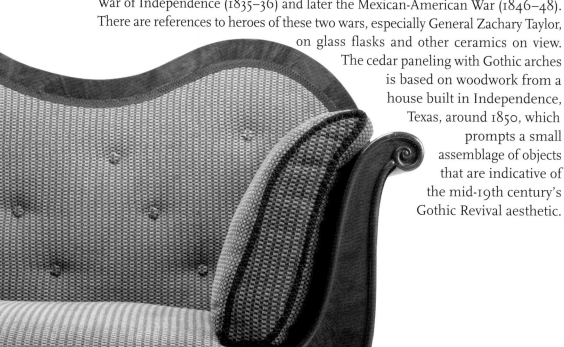

THE TEXAS ALCOVE

The Texas Alcove provides additional space to display Bayou Bend's important collection of mid-19th-century Texas decorative arts. Featured is an imposing wardrobe by Johann Michael Jahn, one of the New Braunfels cabinetmaker's most accomplished pieces. Distinguished by its elegant crest, the wardrobe, or *kleiderschrank*, is a furniture form closely identified with the Biedermeier style that dominated German culture between 1815 and 1850; the restrained designs, utility, and comfort were popular with the middle class. As German immigrants flowed into Texas, so did their tastes. The principal distinction was that the Texas pieces were made with indigenous woods, such as the wardrobe's beautifully grained black walnut.

The alcove displays a significant collection of 19th-century Texas pottery. Beginning in the 1830s, a number of potters traveled from South Carolina and settled in eastern and central Texas, including John M. Wilson, who founded the Guadalupe Pottery about 1857 in Guadalupe County, with the assistance of his slaves. In 1869, after emancipation and the end of the Civil War, several of Wilson's former slaves formed their own pottery firm in a community known as Capote, near Seguin. It was the first African American-owned business in Texas, producing salt-glazed stoneware—most of which is stamped "H. Wilson & Co."

A southern influence is evident
throughout Bayou Bend's formal
gardens and woodland paths.
A dazzling variety of azalea and
camellia bushes graces the property,
along with flowering trees such as
magnolia, crape myrtle, and dogwood.

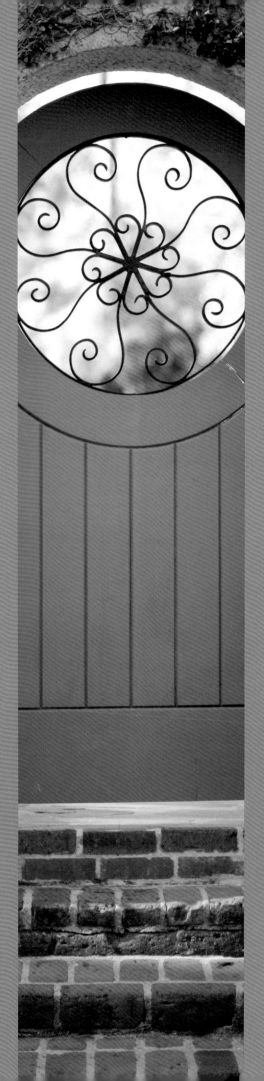

In 1925, Ima Hogg and her brothers Will and Mike selected fourteen acres of natural woodlands and winding ravines along Buffalo Bayou for their home in the newly developed Houston neighborhood of River Oaks. Ima Hogg began planning the surrounding gardens before construction started on the home in 1927.

The gardens at Bayou Bend reflect Miss Hogg's love of beauty, flowers, and nature and her passion for history and all things classical. Her meticulous eye for detail, proportion, and scale and her keen sense of color—all evident in her collection decisions—are also seen in her garden designs. Ima Hogg was admired for her hands-on, experimental approach to gardening. Her continuous personal supervision over nearly forty years resulted in elegant formal gardens and lush woodland trails.

Ima Hogg, Diana Terrace, c. 1974

Ima Hogg and Julia Ideson, East Garden, c. 1935

Bayou Bend's north façade and lawn, c. 1939

Bayou Bend's formal gardens are a rare surviving example of American landscape design popular during the Country Place Era (1890–1940) when the wealthy built mansions surrounded by several acres of gardens on the outskirts of cities. These landscapes include garden "rooms" that seem to extend from the house, water features as focal points, and classical statuary. A sense of proportion, harmony, and restraint is evident throughout. The gardens also reflect what is recognized today as a southern garden renaissance that occurred during the first decades of the 20th century when newly wealthy Southerners built expensive homes surrounded by beautiful gardens featuring southern antebellum plants such as camellia and azalea.

Orpheus and Eurydice performance at Bayou Bend, 1947

Bayou Bend's south facade and driveway, 1950

THE EAST GARDEN

Initially called the Upper Garden, the East Garden extended from the east facade of the house and was the first area laid out and planted at Bayou Bend by 1928. Working with Ima Hogg, Houston landscape architect Ruth London later redesigned the space from 1934 to 1935 as a garden room. Enclosed, private, and formal, the space incorporates elements of English garden design: trees, hedges, lawn, and a water feature. The cast-iron gate behind the octagonal pool and fountain depicts a lyre motif, a classical reference to Miss Hogg's lifelong love of music. Azalea is planted in front of the hedge walls; outside the hedges is 'Duchess de Caze' pink camellia, an early and rare variety from Avery Island in Louisiana. In 1968, the long, narrow center beds were planted with Japanese boxwood, clipped in a scroll design to reflect the ironwork columns on the adjacent East Porch.

THE CLIO GARDEN

Originally called the Lower Garden, the Clio Garden was the second garden to be laid out and planted by Ima Hogg and was completed by 1929. A formal garden of parterre design (meaning low to the ground), it is both ornamental and well-manicured so that the flower beds and paths form a geometric pattern. The boxwood hedges and brick-paved walks emphasize the circular shape of the beds of azalea. Made by the Antonio Frilli Studio in Florence, Italy, the statue of Clio, muse of history, was positioned at the center of the parterre in 1939. The sculpture originally faced the statue of Euterpe across the Diana Garden, but when the gardens opened to the public in 1966, Clio was rotated ninety degrees to provide a more gracious welcome to guests as they cross the suspension bridge. Blue pansies decorate the garden from January through April, and fragrant wisteria blossoms in March and April.

CLIO

THE DIANA GARDEN

Laid out between 1937 and 1939, the Diana Garden best exemplifies the balance of architectural and landscape design at Bayou Bend. The garden's focal point is an Italian marble statue of Diana, Roman goddess of wild animals and the hunt, commissioned by Ima Hogg in 1937. From the main door of the house to the statue is an axis, and a cross axis is created by the Clio and Euterpe gardens. The Diana Garden, with its expansive, terraced lawn, is a model of classical simplicity—an outdoor room defined by walls of evergreen yaupon hedges that separate the garden from the native bayou woodlands. A reflecting pool, positioned before Diana, shoots arching water jets from the fountain. The statue stands before columnar trees of Japanese yew, amid evergreen shrubs and azalea, with crape myrtle on either side.

THE DIANA TERRACE

Designed by the renowned Houston architect John F. Staub, who also designed the mansion, the terrace affords a stunning view of Diana, the fountain and reflecting pool, and the expansive lawn. When the Hogg family moved into Bayou Bend in 1928, the area surrounding the terrace was heavily wooded. As the concept for the Diana Garden evolved, most trees of more than ten inches in diameter were saved. Several large trees were integrated into the garden design, but have since been lost by natural causes. Will Hogg salvaged the terrace's pink flagstones from downtown Houston neighborhoods that were upgrading to modern concrete sidewalks in the 1920s. In 1936, Weber Iron Works of Houston made Ima Hogg cast-iron furniture with a lyre motif, reflecting her love of music. Potted flowers in pink and white, Miss Hogg's favorite colors, and azalea surround the terrace.

THE EUTERPE GARDEN

Created between 1938 and 1939, the Euterpe Garden forms a visual balance to Clio but is less formal. A transitional space between the formal gardens and the surrounding woodlands, this garden is a much looser interpretation of the garden room. As with Clio, Ima Hogg acquired the marble statue of Euterpe, muse of music, from Antonio Frilli in Rome, who copied them from classical pieces in the Vatican Museum. Given Miss Hogg's musical background, Euterpe was an understandable selection. The location of the statue was dictated by the presence of a large double-trunk sycamore and a towering pine tree, which remain in the garden today. The family had demonstrated a reverence for preserving larger trees at the time the house was sited in the mid-1920s, and she continued to retain older trees whenever possible as she developed her gardens.

Euterpe sits in front of columns of Japanese yew, shaded by overhanging branches of pine and oak. At the base of the statue is maidenhair fern flanked by rare azalea planted at Bayou Bend in the 1930s. Redbud, pink oriental magnolia, and Mexican plum trees are planted nearby.

THE CARLA GARDEN

The force of Hurricane Carla in 1961 carved an opening in the woods just south of the Euterpe Garden. Ima Hogg used the destruction to a positive effect, designing a garden-in-the-round in the resulting clearing, originally planned around a large off-center tree (destroyed by Hurricane Alicia in 1983). Landscape architects Janet K. Wagner and Harriet Osborn designed the garden with a semicircular brick patio and retaining wall to help control erosion problems created by hurricanes. Boxwood borders the terrace, and concentric circles of azalea bloom in colors ranging from light to dark pink. According to Miss Hogg's instructions, the garden was designed to allow one to sit on the patio and see the statue of Euterpe below. She playfully placed an antique carousel figure of a bright-colored peacock in the center, which is brought out at the River Oaks Garden Club's annual Azalea Trail. Bayou Bend has been included in the trail every year since it began in 1935.

THE BUTTERFLY GARDEN

Finished in 1942, the Butterfly Garden reflects the parterre design of the Clio Garden. The lighthearted garden is designed with careful symmetry in a forested area. Whimsical brickwork creates the butterfly's body, antennae, and outline of its wings. Hedged by boxwood, the wings are filled with three shades of azalea used to form its stripes. There are about 350 azalea plants, including the rare 'Christmas Cheer' variety. Ima Hogg ornamented the area with a small cupid figure, potted urns, and a pair of iron benches framed by winter-blooming camellia bushes.

THE WHITE GARDEN

Located deep within the woods and surrounded by ravines, the White Garden is the most natural one at Bayou Bend. Completed in 1936, it is entirely green and white, providing a sense of coolness and serenity. Azalea, camellia, gardenia, and dogwood are joined by a rich array of spirea and narcissus throughout the year. In memory of Alvin Wheeler, her devoted gardener for thirty years, Miss Hogg placed two small bronze deer, a plaque, and a bench at the edge of the garden in 1971. She cherished the gardener's role, writing in 1975, "Neither rainfall nor feeding can nourish plant life and flowering things like a gardener's words of praise and love." As a result of the River Oaks Garden Club's 2010 master plan, the White Garden was restored after severe damage from Hurricane Ike in 2008. More than 300 trees were lost at Bayou Bend in one night.

The Woodland Ravines

To the south of the house, this woodland path is a protected area for indigenous plants. Ima Hogg firmly believed in preserving the native environment. The trees, such as tulip poplar, maple, and hornbeam, and the understory growth are a deliberate contrast to the formal gardens. The woods provide a natural progression from a heavily designed environment to a more natural one. Visitors can explore the woods along gravel paths and wooden bridges. Most invasive plants have been removed. The ravines create an undulating landscape and serve to carry off heavy rains to the bayou. When there is a downpour, the water rushes along the ravines and cascades down the waterfalls. Native wildlife thrives in this area, including rabbits, squirrels, cardinals, and mockingbirds.

Lora Jean Kilroy
Visitor and Education Center

Ima Hogg foresaw the need for a visitor and education center shortly after Bayou Bend opened to the public in 1966. Three years later, she purchased additional land to the north specifically for such a facility in the future. Over the subsequent decades, the need for a visitor center grew more pressing as the Museum and its education programming grew. Miss Hogg's vision became a reality in 2010, thanks to dedicated supporters such as Lora Jean Kilroy, the center's lead bene-factor for whom the building is named. A longtime supporter of Bayou Bend and life trustee of the Museum, Mrs. Kilroy and many others continue Ima Hogg's legacy in the 21st century, helping to keep America's early history and cultural heritage alive for generations to come through the objects in the Bayou Bend Collection.

The Lora Jean Kilroy Visitor and Education Center expands Bayou Bend's capacity for programming, outreach, and scholarship in American art. Located in an urban

setting, it welcomes visitors as a modern gateway to Bayou Bend. The contemporary building provides an intentional contrast to the historic estate and its distinguished collections that guests discover just down a hill and across a bridge. Designed by Houston architect Leslie Elkins, the 18,000-square-foot building achieved LEED-Silver certification for its environmentally sensitive construction and energy efficiency. The Houston landscape firm of McDugald-Steele designed the center's two acres of grounds as a modern complement to Bayou Bend's historic gardens. Guests begin their visit in the T.L.L. Temple Foundation Orientation Gallery, where they are introduced to Bayou Bend Collection and Gardens through three five-minute videos shown on a dramatic thirteen-foot-long media wall and a timeline that surveys the stylistic periods represented in the collection. The adjacent Hogg Family Legacy Room celebrates the family's deep commitment to civic responsibility and their vision of Houston as a metropolis of international importance.

KITTY KING POWELL LIBRARY AND STUDY CENTER

The Kitty King Powell Library and Study Center is located on the second floor of the Kilroy Center. The library houses thousands of volumes on 17th- to 19th-century American decorative arts, material culture, and art. Special collections include rare cabinetmaker design books and the Hogg Family Collection of books. Open to the public, the library serves as an important resource for scholars, staff, docents, and volunteers, and was made possible thanks to a major gift from former Bayou Bend docent Kitty King Powell.

In conjunction with the library, the William J. Hill Texas Artisans and Artists Archive was established in 2011 with a major gift from Mr. Hill, a Houston philanthropist. The archive fosters research in the field of Texas material culture through a major, searchable Internet database that documents the lives, work, business practices, and products of artisans and artists working in Texas in the 19th century. The goal of the ever-growing digital archive is to encourage new research while focusing greater attention on Texas contributions to the history of American decorative arts, as well as painting, photography, and other media.

THE SHOP AT BAYOU BEND

The Kilroy Center lobby opens onto The Shop at Bayou Bend. Visitors enjoy a memorable retail experience in a boutique atmosphere, selecting from a range of unique gifts that reflects the quality, craftsmanship, and beauty of the collection and gardens. The Shop features many custom-made items that are available exclusively at Bayou Bend. Especially popular are vases and bowls made from wood salvaged from trees on Bayou Bend's historic property. Proceeds from purchases support Bayou Bend's operations and programs.

Support Groups

In preparation of Bayou Bend's public opening in 1961, Ima Hogg invited
a group of women to attend a training class to be docent interpreters. Today,
more than 200 dedicated women and men are members of the Bayou Bend
Docent Organization, one of the most respected docent groups in America.
Donating their time and expertise, they lead tours of the house and interpret
the collection through ongoing scholarship and public lectures. The docents
also support much of the collection through contributions to their named
accessions endowment fund.

Miss Hogg joined the River Oaks Garden Club when it was founded in 1927,
and her gardens have been featured on every Azalea Trail since its inception
in 1936. In 1961, she invited the club to assume permanent supervision of
the grounds, and in 1967 it established the Bayou Bend Gardens Endowment
Fund to assure the gardens' continued state of excellence. In keeping with Miss
Hogg's original vision, members oversee long-range planning for the gardens,
arrange fresh flowers for the downstairs rooms, assist the garden's professional
staff, and provide financial support for annual operations of the gardens.

Two other groups of volunteers generously lend their support and time to Bayou Bend. In 1968, Miss Hogg asked the Houston Junior Woman's Club to provide volunteers to welcome visitors one Sunday a month to a free Family Day. Through this partnership, thousands of children and adults have explored the downstairs rooms and gardens, and enjoyed activities that bring the past to life with music, costume, and crafts. The club's annual fundraiser helps support Bayou Bend's education programs as well as helps the collection through grants to their named accessions endowment fund.

First presidents of Houston Junior Woman's Club, c. 1976

Founded in 1952 by Kappa Alpha Theta Houston alumnae, the Theta Charity Antiques Show is one of the nation's outstanding gatherings of arts and antiques dealers and has generously included Bayou Bend as a beneficiary since 1969. Ima Hogg had been an early and enthusiastic champion of the show. Over the decades, the Theta funds have made it possible to acquire many important objects for the collection, helping to celebrate the nation's rich history and cultural achievements.

Theta members at 50th anniversary Theta Charity Antiques Show, 2002

PHOTO CREDITS

Images of the house and gardens on the front cover, back cover, and interior of book are by Rick Gardner; Rick Gardner in memory of Mary Gardner; Phil Grant; and Justin Nguyen.

The decorative arts and paintings pictured throughout this publication are in the Bayou Bend Collection. Photographs are by Thomas R. DuBrock and Rick Gardner. For more information, please visit the Museum's website www.mfah.org/bayoubend or call 713.639.7750 to be connected to the curatorial department for assistance.

The following images are from the Archives of the Museum of Fine Arts, Houston: Hogg family children, MS21-038 (p. 8); Ima Hogg, MS07-001 (p. 10); Patton Place (now Varner-Hogg Plantation), MS2114-008-007 (p. 10); Oil field, West Columbia, RG36-351 (p. 10); Ima Hogg and Wayne Bell, Winedale Historical Center, MS21-196-001 (p. 11); Ima Hogg, MS21-047 (p. 11); John F. Staub, RG35-067-001 (p. 13); Ima Hogg and River Oaks Garden Club members, Clio Garden, MS21-214-001 (p. 13); Library (now Pine Room), MS21-033 (p. 14); First docent class, Ima Hogg and Jonathan Fairbanks, Philadelphia Hall, MS21-057 (p. 14); Ima Hogg, Katharine Prentis Murphy, and John Staub, Murphy Room, MS21-056-001 (p. 14); Ima Hogg at dedication of Bayou Bend, MS21-184-020 (p. 15); Ima Hogg and David B. Warren, MS21-070-001 (p. 15); Ima Hogg, MS81-001 (p. 15); Ima Hogg, Diana Terrace, MS21-068 (p. 72); Ima Hogg and Julia Ideson, East Garden, MS21-217-001 (p. 72); Bayou Bend's north facade and lawn, MS21-218 (p. 72); *Orpheus and Eurydice* performance at Bayou Bend, MS2114-001 (p. 73); Bayou Bend's south facade and driveway, MS21-202 (p. 73); Ima Hogg with Bayou Bend docents on south steps, RG35-064 (p. 98); and River Oaks Garden Club members in Bayou Bend's gardens, MS22-025-001 (p. 98).

The following images are from The Dolph Briscoe Center for American History, The University of Texas at Austin: The Hogg family, (p. 8); Joseph Lewis Hogg (p. 9); Ima Hogg, (p. 10); and *Houston Post-Dispatch*, (p. 13).

The following images are from the Austin History Center, Austin Public Library: Texas Governor's Mansion, PICA 06530 (p. 10); and Ima Hogg (right) in parade, Austin, PICA 03084 (p. 10).

The following images are in various collections: Houston Symphony meeting, Bayou Bend, courtesy of Greater Houston Partnership (p. 11); Hogg Foundation publication, courtesy of Hogg Foundation for Mental Health (p. 11); Office interior, Hogg Brothers, Houston, MSS 0019-813, Houston Public Library, HMRC (p. 12); Plan of River Oaks, courtesy of River Oaks Property Owners, Inc., Houston, photography by Rick Gardner (p. 13); *Houston Chronicle*, courtesy of the newspaper (p. 14); First eight presidents of Houston Junior Woman's Club, Betty Jukes, the group's founder, stands in the center, courtesy of Nancy Grant (p. 99); and Mary Frances Couper, Martha Taylor Jones, and Mary Margaret McDonald at the 50th anniversary Theta Charity Antiques Show, courtesy of Martha Taylor Jones (p. 99).

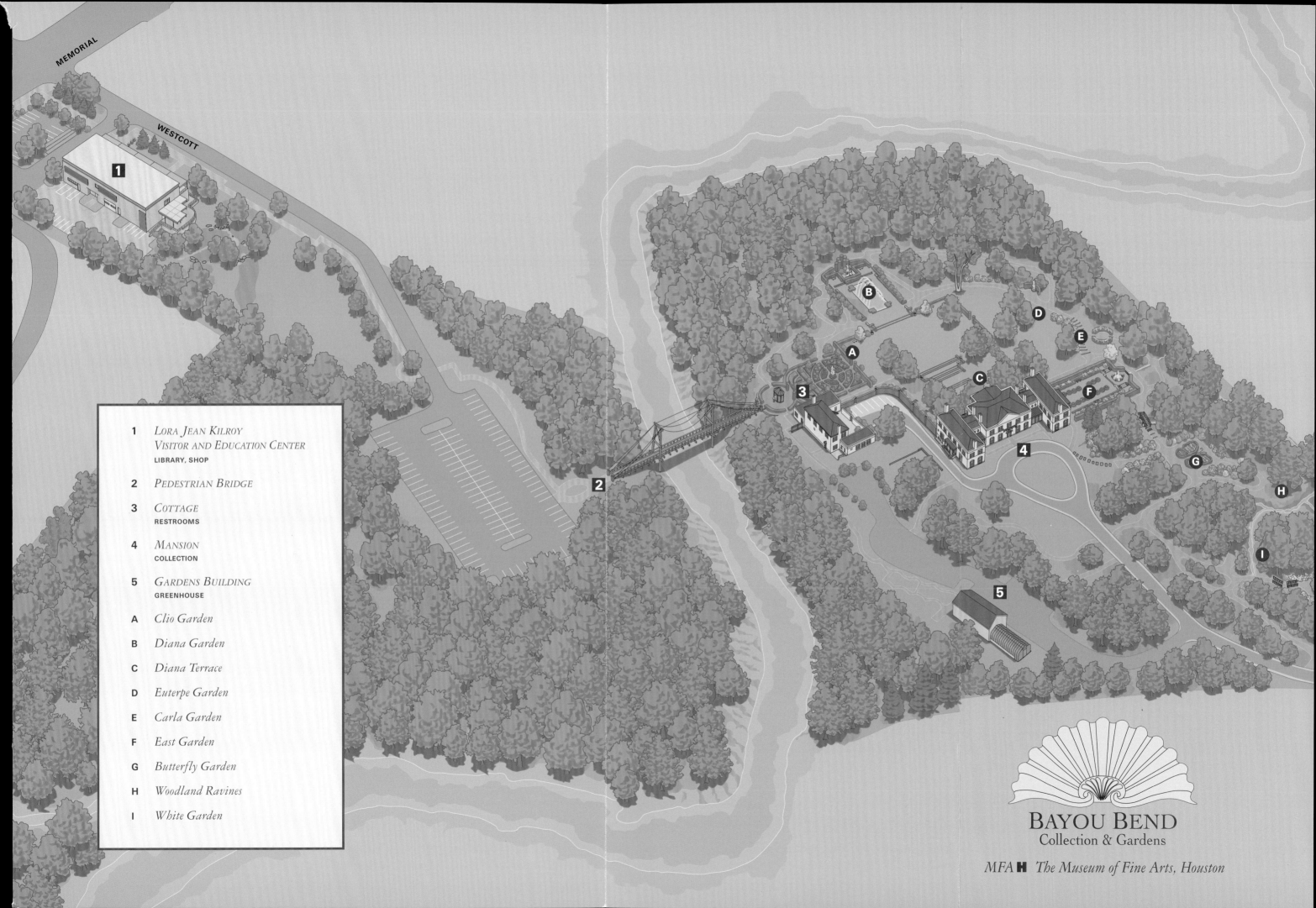

MEMORIAL

WESTCOTT

1

2

3

A

B

C

D

E

F

4

5

G

H

I

1 *LORA JEAN KILROY*
VISITOR AND EDUCATION CENTER
LIBRARY, SHOP

2 *PEDESTRIAN BRIDGE*

3 *COTTAGE*
RESTROOMS

4 *MANSION*
COLLECTION

5 *GARDENS BUILDING*
GREENHOUSE

A *Clio Garden*

B *Diana Garden*

C *Diana Terrace*

D *Euterpe Garden*

E *Carla Garden*

F *East Garden*

G *Butterfly Garden*

H *Woodland Ravines*

I *White Garden*

BAYOU BEND
Collection & Gardens

MFA **H** *The Museum of Fine Arts, Houston*